# WHO LIVES IN THIS MEADOW?

## A Story of Animal Life

**GLENN O. BLOUGH**

**PICTURES BY
JEANNE BENDICK**

*Purple House Press*   *Kentucky*

WRITTEN IN 1961 BY GLENN BLOUGH
COPYRIGHT © 2021 BY PURPLE HOUSE PRESS
ISBN 9781948959582 (hc) 9781948959599 (pb)

## LOOK INTO A MEADOW

I think you will like this meadow. You can see it from the road that passes by. You can see it better if you look over the gate where the cows go in. You can see it best if you open the gate and walk in. That is the best way to explore a meadow.

A fence goes all the way around the meadow. It keeps the cows in and other large animals out. Rabbits and cats and dogs and ducks and other small animals can go right through the fence. They come in when they want to and go out when they want to.

Bushes and small trees grow along the fence. The ground in the meadow is covered with green grass and red clover and white clover and a few flowers. There is a pond in the middle of the meadow and there is a large, old dead tree at the edge of the pond.

You would probably say that the meadow is beautiful. If the animals that live there could talk they might say, "This is a fine place for us to live." A scientist who knows many things about animals would call the meadow a good *environment* for the animals that live there. That means that the animals have a good place for making homes, for taking care of their families, for finding their food, and for all of the other things they do.

This is a book about how the animals get along in their meadow environment. When you explore the meadow you will see that the animals are built just right for living there.

The meadow is quiet except sometimes you can hear the water in the brook. It trickles. Sometimes you can hear the meadowlark that sits on the fence. It whistles. Sometimes you can hear the kingfisher that sits on a branch of that old dead tree. It rattles.

When the meadowlark sings it makes you feel like trying to whistle its song. But when the kingfisher rattles, you wouldn't think of whistling. The kingfisher is not a very musical bird. Sometimes you hear a red-headed woodpecker on that old dead tree. It goes rap-tap, rap-tap. Sometimes in spring you hear frogs croaking in the pond. They croak loud enough to be heard across the road. Except for the soft trickles, the merry whistles, the rattles and the croaks, the meadow is a quiet place.

Sometimes, if you are a good listener, you can hear the bumblebees buzzing in the red clover. You must stand very quietly and listen as hard as you can. But no matter how hard you try you can't hear the mice and the moles that live in the ground. You can't hear the fish that live in the water. They don't make sounds that you can hear. Neither do the turtles that sit beside the pond, nor the rabbits that frolic in the grass. They all live quietly in the meadow.

If the clover in the meadow is in blossom and the wind blows toward you, you can smell the sweetness in the air. When rain falls on the meadow you can see new greenness in the grass. When the sun shines you can see the drops of water sparkle.

The animals in the meadow are busy going here and there. Some of them dig in the ground. Some creep or crawl over it. Some climb trees. Some hop. Some fly through the air. And some just run over the ground to get from where they are to where they want to be.

The animals in the meadow are great eaters. Some nibble. Some gnaw. Some chew. Some sip. Some lap. And some just bite into the things which they eat when they are hungry. The animals in the meadow are great hunters too. The kingfisher hunts. So do the fish and the ducks and the moles and the hawks.

The animals live in many different kinds of environments. Some live in the water of the pond and brook. Water is a good environment for them. You will discover why this is true if you watch them.

Let's look down into the water of the pond.

# LIVING UNDER THE WATER

Some animals live near the pond and just go into it now and then. Toads and turtles do that. Some live on top of the water and find food in it. Ducks do that. Some live under the water and never come into the meadow at all. Fish do that.

Animals that live underwater must be able to breathe under the water and, of course, they must be able to swim. They must be able to get food and to get away from their enemies. If you look carefully at a fish or another water animal, you might say, "This animal is built for living in the water." If animals that live in the water could talk, they might say, "We like it here!" A scientist would say, "These animals are adapted to their environment." That means that they are especially fitted to live where they do.

Let's see how a fish is adapted to live underwater. First let's see how it gets air. The fish has no lungs. It couldn't use lungs underwater if it had them.

A fish breathes with gills. It takes water into its mouth. This water has air in it. The water goes out over the gills that are on the sides of the fish's head. The gills take the oxygen out of the air that is in the water. When you see a fish opening and closing its mouth, the fish is not drinking, it is breathing. It does not swallow water. The water goes in its mouth and then goes out over its gills. The gills take the oxygen out of the water. Animals that live under the water for very long must use gills for breathing.

The turtle can go underwater and stay for quite a while, but sooner or later it must come up for air. Frogs can stay underwater for quite a while too. But sooner or later they, also, must come up for air. Turtles and frogs have lungs for breathing. They do not have gills.

There are other things about a fish that show you that it is adapted to its environment. It has just the right shape to move easily through the water. It is pointed in the front. It is not very thick in the middle. And it is pointed at the back. This makes pushing through the water very easy.

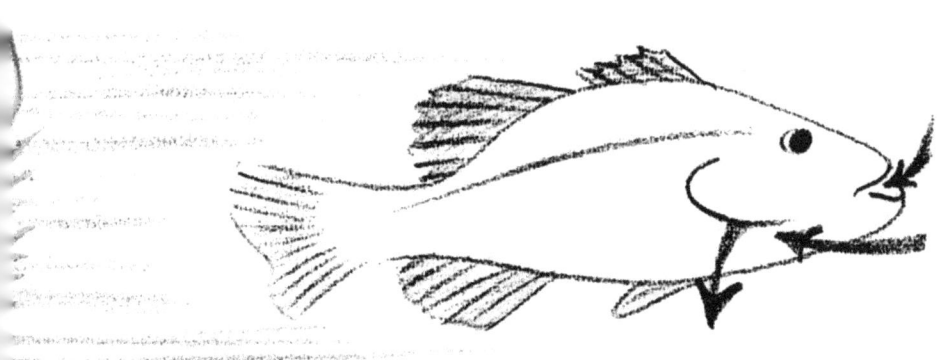

WATER GOES INTO THE FISH'S MOUTH, PASSES OVER ITS GILLS AND COMES OUT HERE. THE GILLS TAKE OXYGEN OUT OF THE WATER.

If you have ever tried to hold a fish in your hand you know something else that helps it swim. The fish is very slippery. This makes going through the water very easy. The fish uses fins for swimming. There are fins on the side of its body and on the top and on the bottom. The tail is a very important fin too. When the tail wags back and forth in the water, the fish moves ahead. The other fins help the fish to turn around and go up and down. The pointed, slippery, finny fish is certainly well adapted to its environment, wouldn't you say?

THE FINS ON THE TOP, BOTTOM AND SIDES HELP THE FISH TURN AND GO UP AND DOWN

THE TAIL FIN PUSHES THE FISH AHEAD

There are crayfish in the pond. They breathe with gills too. But they are not built very much like a fish. Some people call crayfish, *crawdads*. But no matter what you call them, they are fun to watch and especially well adapted to their environment.

The crayfish that lives in the pond is a better swimmer than you might think. It has so many legs you might think that it is clumsy, but it doesn't use its legs for swimming. Look at that flipper tail. It is usually folded under the crayfish. But when the crayfish flips its tail out, this pushes it through the water like lightning. A crayfish can go forward and backward.

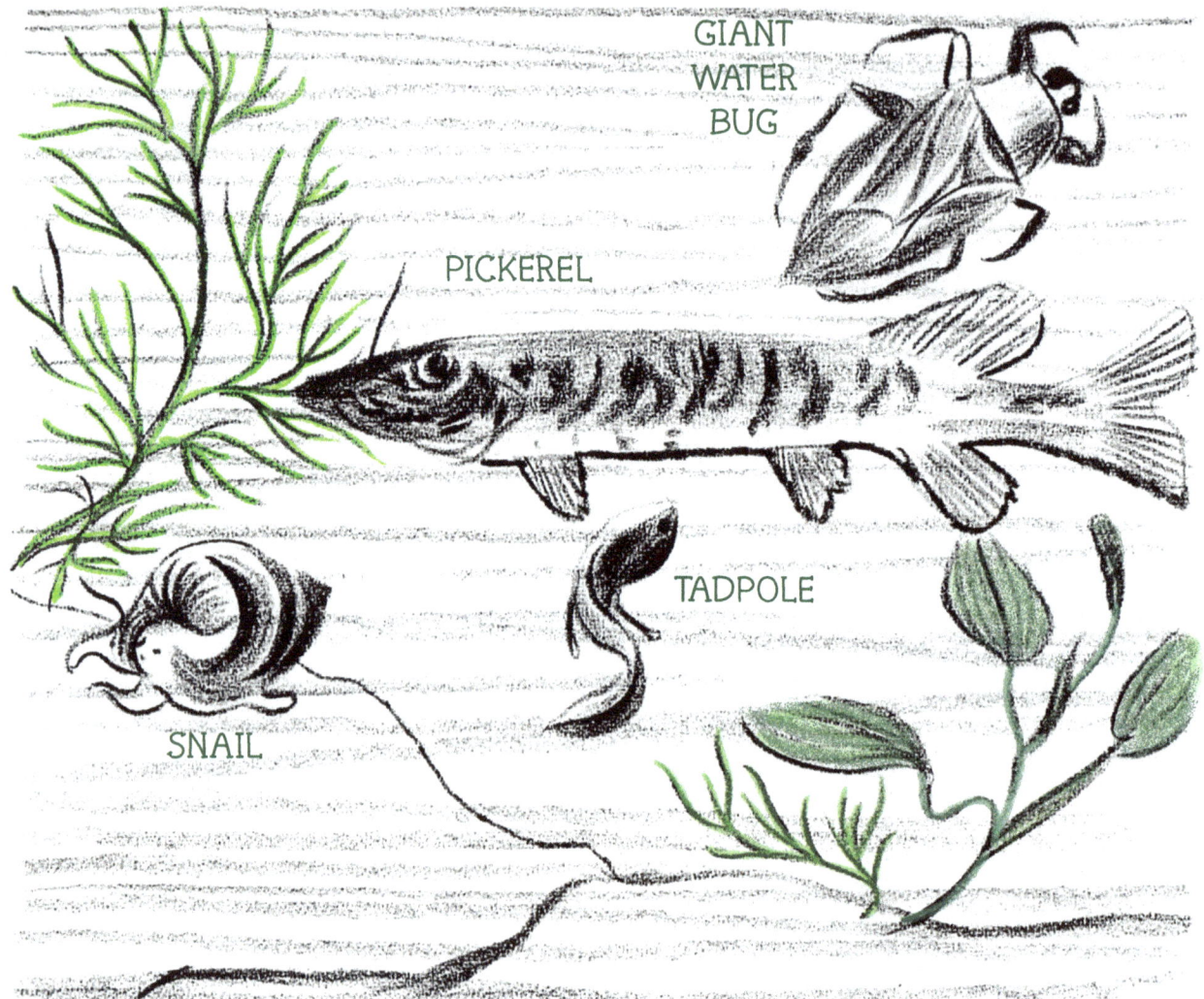

## YOU MIGHT FIND THESE ANIMALS IN A POND TOO

GIANT WATER BUG

PICKEREL

TADPOLE

SNAIL

The water in the pond in the meadow is a fine place for animals that are adapted for living there. If you go exploring in other ponds, you may find other kinds of animals living there. If you watch these animals you will see that they are all adapted for living in a water environment.

Some animals are adapted for living on the water, but not under it. There are many of them in this meadow. Shall we explore to see what they are?

# LIVING ON THE WATER

Living *on* the water is not like living *under* it. The white ducks that slip over the pond in the meadow are especially adapted for floating on water, for swimming in it, and for eating from the bottom of it. But they can't live under the water as fish do.

You have heard of water running off a duck's back. You should see this sometime. When rain falls on ducks, or when they dive into the water, or if something splashes water on them, ducks just shake themselves and their feathers are dry. Water runs off their feathers even better than it does from a raincoat. Their feathers have oil on them. This keeps the water from soaking in and helps the ducks to float. They couldn't do the things they do if the water soaked into their feathers. If it did, the ducks would get heavy and sink to the bottom of the pond. And that is a good place for a fish but not for a duck.

A DUCK HAS A COATING OF OIL ON ITS FEATHERS

The white duck's feet are especially good for swimming. They are set back under its body and the toes have a web of skin between them. This makes them perfect for paddling. The duck spreads out its toes and the web of skin pushes against the water and away goes the duck across the pond. The duck's feet are good for turning and diving too. Watch sometime and you will see. Ducks can even swim underwater and they sometimes do. Sometimes when you are watching the white ducks in the pond, you see only their tails sticking out of the water. The ducks are looking for food in the water. But they must soon come to the top of the pond to get air.

A DUCK'S FOOT IS MADE LIKE THIS

No wonder the ducks are so much at home in the pond. They are built just right for moving about in it and for getting food out of it. They are very well adapted for life on the water.

Many other animals are adapted for swimming. Turtles are. Frogs and toads are. Watch them in the water and you will see.

# LIVING UNDER THE GROUND

Some animals can live under the ground in the meadow. Ground moles can. If you explore in this meadow you would know that moles live here. They push up the dirt when they make their tunnels under the ground. You can see where the mole's tunnel goes if you follow the pushed-up dirt. One mole tunnel begins by the fence gate and twists around until it ends by the fence, near the tree where the woodpecker pecks and the kingfisher fishes. You can look and look and never find the door of the tunnel. The mole doesn't come up into the meadow very often.

You can tell by looking at a mole that it is adapted for living under the ground. A mole's body is built for tunnelmaking. The mole is small. Its fur is short. The mole is only about nine inches long if you count its tail, which is about an inch long. Its legs are short. What in the world would a mole do with long legs down in the underground tunnel? The mole's front feet are short and they look a little like flat paddles. They have strong

claws and are perfect for digging underground. The mole's nose is pointed and it has a short neck.

There's no light down in the ground and the mole hasn't much use for eyes. Its eyes are very, very tiny. They are hardly larger than a pinhead and are no good for seeing. The mole doesn't need to see. If its eyes were large the mole would probably get dirt in them anyway.

There are not many sounds down in the ground and the mole hasn't much use for ears. Its ears do not show on the outside of its head at all. If they did, all sorts of things could happen to them while the mole is making a tunnel and living under the ground. You can see that the short-furred, pointed-noised, short-legged mole is built just right for a home under the ground in the meadow.

If you explore under the ground in other meadows you will find other animals—ants and beetles and woodchucks and earthworms. Keep exploring and you'll find still more. Many animals are adapted for living under the ground.

ANTS AND WOODCHUCKS LIVE IN MEADOWS TOO

## FLYING THROUGH THE AIR

The hawk that sometimes circles over the meadow is a beautiful flyer. When it flies over the meadow, the rabbits and field mice run and hide. The ducks start up such a quacking as you never heard before. Many animals are afraid of hawks.

The hawk is especially well built for flying. It can sail around high in the air and glide with the wind. It can dive to the earth when it's looking for food. Then the hawk can zoom up into the air with a rabbit or a field mouse or some other animal it likes to eat. A hawk's wing has long strong feathers and it has strong muscles to move its wings.

But long, strong wings are not the only parts of the hawk's body that fit its life. A hawk's feet have the sharpest,

strongest claws you ever saw. How else could a hawk grab onto an animal and hold it? For mouse-eating, a beak like the red-headed woodpecker's wouldn't be any good at all. But the hawk is built for meat-eating. Its beak is sharp as a knife and has a sharp hook on it. The beak can tear and rip. And it does. How else could the hawk eat the animals it catches?

There are many kinds of hawks and they eat many different kinds of animals. There are red-tailed hawks, and sharp-shinned hawks, and other kinds. Some are helpful. A few are harmful. Most kinds of hawks eat mice and other animals that are harmful because they eat corn and other seeds that we use for food. But some hawks may eat chickens. They are harmful hawks. You need to know what kind of hawk is flying over the meadow before you can tell if it is a helpful hawk or a harmful hawk. And you need to know what food the hawk eats.

DIFFERENT KINDS OF HAWKS HAVE DIFFERENT SHAPES

SOARING HAWKS HAVE BROAD WINGS AND TAILS

FALCONS HAVE POINTED WINGS

LOW-FLYING HAWKS HAVE ROUND WINGS AND LONG TAILS

But no matter what kind of a bird you see, all birds are adapted to their environment. They are all adapted to get and eat the special food they like. Some birds are adapted to eat seeds. They have strong beaks. Some eat insects. Their beaks are just the right size and shape for eating insects. Woodpeckers have beaks that are especially adapted to get insects. Can you guess how?

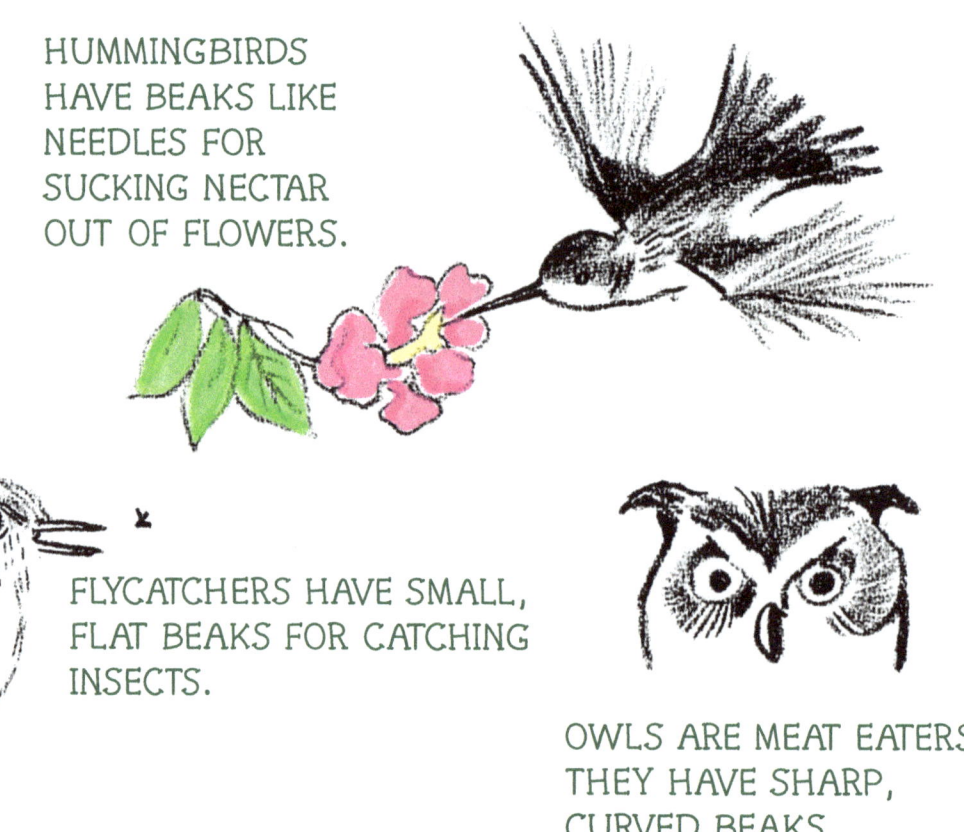

HUMMINGBIRDS HAVE BEAKS LIKE NEEDLES FOR SUCKING NECTAR OUT OF FLOWERS.

FLYCATCHERS HAVE SMALL, FLAT BEAKS FOR CATCHING INSECTS.

OWLS ARE MEAT EATERS. THEY HAVE SHARP, CURVED BEAKS.

FINCHES ARE SEED EATERS. THEY HAVE SHORT, STRONG BEAKS.

# HUNTING AND EATING

Animals are almost always hungry and are adapted for hunting and eating in many different ways. If you watch them you may discover some of these ways. Some of them will surprise you.

# THE RED-HEADED WOODPECKER

When you see the red-headed woodpecker on the old dead tree it is probably hunting for something to eat. A woodpecker is adapted for hunting and eating from tongue to tail. You never see it sitting on a telephone wire and it's not easy for a woodpecker to sit on the ground. But sitting on a side of a tree is easy. The woodpecker's foot has four toes. Two point to the front, two point to the back. All four toes have sharp claws. This two-to-the-front and two-to-the-back is fine for climbing over the bark, up and down trees, around the branches, and all over the outside of the tree.

A LONG WAY OFF IN THE WOODS YOU CAN HEAR A WOODPECKER

The red-headed woodpecker has been up and down and around that old dead tree by the pond more times than you can count. It hunts for insects and insect eggs in the bark and cracks of that old dead tree. Its sharp claws are a great help, but if you watch you'll see that the woodpecker's tail is very helpful too. The feathers at the end of its tail are stiff and sharp. This makes them especially handy for the woodpecker to prop itself against the bark of the old dead tree while it's creeping around.

If you go exploring, you may hear that red-headed woodpecker rap-tap, rap-tap, on that old dead tree. If you are not too noisy, you can get very close. You can see its head go back and forth as fast as a pinwheel in the wind and you can see its sharp pointed beak drive into the bark.

But you can stand right under that dead tree and watch the woodpecker and never know about its remarkably handy, long tongue. The woodpecker can stick it out quite far, and it has barbs on the end something like the barb on a fish hook. When the woodpecker has pecked away the bark and found a tasty insect inside, it sticks out that long tongue with the barbs on it. The woodpecker's tongue hooks into the insect, then its tongue is pulled out of the bark into its mouth and there goes the insect. That is the last you'll ever see of it. That's why we say the red-headed woodpecker is adapted for life from tongue to tail. So are downy and hairy woodpeckers. Watch a bird eat seeds. Watch a bird eat insects. You will see how important the shape of its beak is.

Woodpeckers have no teeth. Neither do other birds, but their beaks are especially built to help them eat the kind of foods they eat. They don't need teeth.

While the red-headed woodpecker is rap-tap-tapping on that old dead tree another bird is using the tree for a hunting perch. The bird is a kingfisher.

## THE KINGFISHER

When you look more than once at the kingfisher, you begin to make some discoveries. The kingfisher is quite a bird. But it can't do what the woodpecker does—not at all. It can't do what the hawk does—not at all. It can't do what the duck does. It certainly can't. If it could do these things, it wouldn't be a kingfisher.

Sometimes the kingfisher sits on the old dead tree by the pond for a long time. You might think that it is just sitting. But it isn't. The kingfisher is hunting. All at once you'll see it plop down on the water and fly up with a fish in its mouth. How can it do this? A kingfisher's eyes are especially good at looking for fish. It can see things that are quite far away and it can see things that are nearby too. A kingfisher's beak is especially good for grabbing a fish and so are its claws. Its beak is long and pointed and strong. The end of it is sharp. The kingfisher's claws are sharp and fine for grabbing hold of fish and other food to eat.

Sometimes even with good eyes and a strong sharp beak the kingfisher doesn't catch the fish it is after. It sometimes misses and then flies back to the perch on the old dead tree and tries again. It catches enough fish and frogs and tadpoles and crayfish to satisfy its appetite. That's enough for a kingfisher.

While the red-headed woodpecker is rap-tap-tapping on the old dead tree and the kingfisher is fishing from its branches, another bird is looking for fish in the pond. But this bird hunts in quite a different way.

## THE GREAT BLUE HERON

The great blue heron is not bright blue like the sky on a sunny day or the blue in the flag. It is more like the color of an overcast sky or of a blackboard that's dusty.

The great blue heron's long legs are fine for walking slowly in the water. The toes are not webbed like the duck's toes. The heron doesn't swim for its food. It walks along quietly on its long legs. It lifts one leg up and then puts it down quietly in the water and then does the same with the other leg. The heron stops and looks into the water. All of a sudden the long beak shoots into the water and up comes a wiggling fish—or a crayfish—or a frog or something else that tastes good to a great blue heron. If the blue heron misses, it tries again.

The long, sharp, pointed beak is just right for reaching down into the water. The long legs are just right for wading in the water. The great blue heron is built especially for fishing in water that's not very deep.

That's something a red-headed woodpecker can't do—neither can the hawk. Many birds can't. They are not adapted for getting their food that way. Go exploring near the water sometime and you may find some other birds that have long legs and long, sharp pointed beaks.

## THE BAT

The woodpecker and the kingfisher are not the only animals that use the old dead tree. There is a big hole in the tree and there are animals living in it. They only come out at night. They are little brown bats.

Bats can fly but they are not birds. They have wings, but they have no feathers. They are fur-wearers.

If you took a good look at a bat's wing you would discover that it is built just right for hanging upside down! Each wing has a tiny strong, sharp hook that the bat can latch into any rough place and hang on. These sharp hooks are fine for climbing too. Bats can climb fast.

Those hooks are not the only remarkable parts of a bat's wing. The wings have a thin skin stretched between long stiff bones. This makes the bat's wings fine for flying. The back part of the wing is fastened together and makes a scoop. As the bat flits over the meadow in the evening it scoops up mosquitoes and other insects and eats them.

A bat's eyes are not very good, but its voice helps the bat to know where it is. When its flying, the bat makes a very loud high sound. You couldn't hear the sound even if you were close to the bat. But the bat can hear it. The way the sounds strikes things and bounces back helps the bat to know how close it is to things. The bat uses the echo of its voice as a guide.

Bats are not built for living in tunnels as moles are. They don't need to be because they don't live in tunnels. They are built just right for flying at night to catch insects and then for hanging themselves up in the daytime.

The cat is another fur-wearer that is a good hunter. Sometimes the cat hunts in the daytime and sometimes at night. It can go through the fence and through the gate without opening it. The cat really lives at a nearby farmhouse and only comes to the meadow to hunt.

## THE CAT AND THE RABBIT

The bat and the cat are hardly alike at all except that they are both fur-wearers. They certainly couldn't change places. The cat couldn't possibly hang itself upside down inside that dead tree, and the bat couldn't possibly prowl around the ground of the meadow and catch a mouse. And if the bat could catch a mouse, the bat couldn't eat it. A bat is not built for eating a mouse, but a cat is.

It's hard to hear the cat walk in the meadow. If you look at its feet you will see that they are padded. This helps the cat walk very softly. This helps it get very close to the mouse without being heard.

A cat can easily eat a rat or a mouse or other meat or fish. Its teeth are especially built for eating meat. They are sharp. They are pointed. That's the way meat-eating animals' teeth are built. They need to be sharp and pointed so they can catch their food and hold onto it and rip it apart. A

meat-eating animal's teeth are not like the teeth of an animal that eats plants.

The rabbits in the meadow are not meat eaters. They are plant eaters. A rabbit's teeth are built for nibbling and gnawing like a squirrel's teeth. In the front of its mouth there are two long sharp teeth on the upper jaw and two long sharp teeth on the lower jaw. With these, the rabbit can nibble off grass and gnaw at hard things like the bark of a tree. In the back of the rabbit's mouth are flat teeth for grinding food before it is swallowed. Mice have teeth like that, too. So do beavers and squirrels and muskrats. They are all plant eaters. Many people can tell what kind of food an animal eats by looking at its teeth.

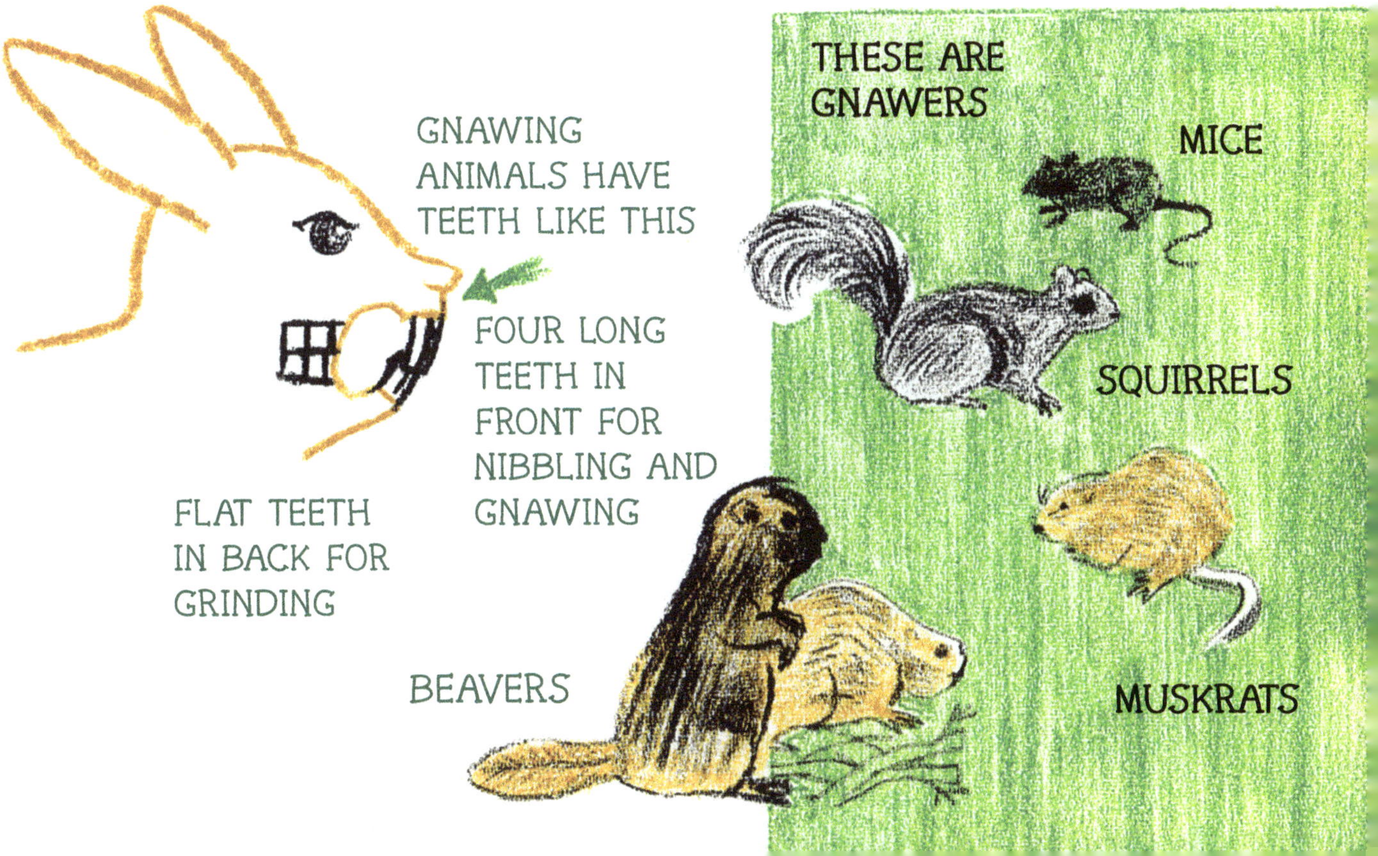

GNAWING ANIMALS HAVE TEETH LIKE THIS

FOUR LONG TEETH IN FRONT FOR NIBBLING AND GNAWING

FLAT TEETH IN BACK FOR GRINDING

THESE ARE GNAWERS

MICE

SQUIRRELS

BEAVERS

MUSKRATS

# ESCAPING FROM ENEMIES

Sometimes when the fish in the water is looking for an insect to eat, the kingfisher is looking for the fish. When the crayfish is looking for some fish eggs to eat, the great blue heron is looking for the crayfish. While the cat is pussyfooting over the meadow looking for a wild mouse, the hawk may be flying overhead looking for the cat. All of these animals need some special ways to keep their enemies from finding them and eating them.

The hawks that fly over the meadow are often looking for the rabbits that live there. When the rabbits are just looking for food and paying attention to their own business, they hop about over the grass. But when they know that the hawk is circling overhead they don't stop to hop. They run and sometimes bound over the ground. When this happens all you can see is that white puff of a tail bounding over the ground. If you can see that far you will finally see the tail disappear under the bushes over by the fence.

If you have ever looked at a rabbit's hind legs you know they are built especially for jumping and running fast. The lower part of the rabbit's hind legs is long. The upper part is short. This makes the legs just right for running and jumping. This often brings good luck to the rabbit because it gets away from enemies. But carrying a rabbit's paw in your pocket won't bring you good luck. People just say that for the fun of it.

Sometimes the rabbit in the meadow doesn't run away at all if you walk near it. The rabbit just sits there and looks so much like the brown meadow grass that you can look right at it and never see it at all. Its color fits into the place where it is sitting. You could even take a picture of the place where the rabbit is sitting and maybe not even know that you have taken a picture of it. The rabbit sometimes just sits when the hawk flies over. But if the rabbit gets too scared it bounds away to safety.

Some of the other animals in the meadow look like the place where they live too. The meadowlark looks like the ground and like the brown grass. When the meadowlark is sitting on its nest in the grass you might look right at it and never see it.

THE RABBIT LOOKS
LIKE THE BROWN GRASS

SO DO THE MEADOWLARK
AND THE FIELD MOUSE

MANY SNAKES LOOK
LIKE GRASS OR
GROUND OR LEAVES

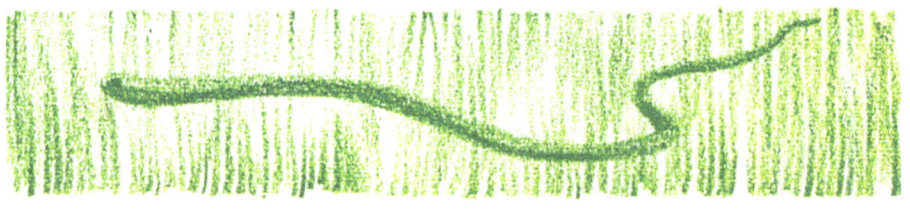

Some of the fish in the pond are hard to see too. They look like the bottom of the pond. This helps them to escape from their enemies. They can swim fast too. You know this if you have ever tried to catch one.

Some animals fight to protect themselves. The cat scratches and bites if another animal tries to harm it. Many other animals use their claws and teeth to protect themselves.

SHREWS ARE VERY TINY, BUT THEY ARE FIERCE FIGHTERS. THEY USE TEETH AND CLAWS.

MUSKRATS HAVE SHARP TEETH AND CLAWS.

The turtle that lives near the pond has a fine way to protect itself. The turtle just pulls its head and its legs and its tail inside its shell and sits there. One day a dog saw it moving slowly along the edge of the pond, the way turtles do. The dog came over and sniffed at the turtle. By the time the dog got there all it could see was the turtle's shell. It turned the turtle over and sniffed. But the turtle didn't move. Soon the dog went away to look at something else, and the turtle stuck out its head and stuck out its legs and then it turned over and away it went. But the turtle didn't go very fast. Who ever saw a turtle hurry? Although it can't get away from danger in a hurry, the turtle's shell protects it very well.

Not all of the animals in the meadow can escape from their enemies. All of the insects cannot escape from the birds that eat them. The woodpeckers eat hundreds of insects and insect eggs. Meadowlarks eat hundreds and hundreds of insects. Other birds in the meadow eat many insects too.

You might think that the woodpeckers and other birds would eat all of the insects in the meadow. But they don't. Do you know why? It's because there are so many insects. Every year each mother insect lays more eggs than you can count. All sorts of things can happen to the eggs but there are still plenty left to hatch. All sorts of things can happen to the insects that hatch, and yet there are plenty left to grow and lay more eggs to hatch more insects, to lay more eggs and so on and on.

GRASSHOPPERS LAY THEIR EGGS RIGHT UNDER THE SOIL

SPITTLEBUGS LAY THEIR EGGS ON GRASS OR PLANT STEMS

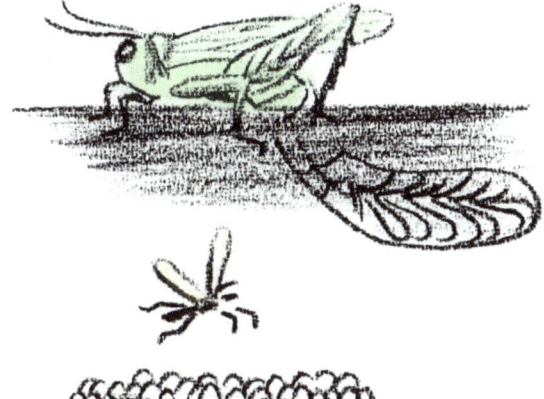

MOSQUITOES LAY THEIR EGGS ON STILL WATER

INSECTS LAY MILLIONS AND MILLIONS OF EGGS

You might think that the crayfish would soon be gone from the pond in the meadow because the fish and other animals eat the crayfish's eggs. But the mother crayfish lays plenty of eggs. All sorts of things can happen to the eggs but there are still plenty left to hatch. The kingfisher and the blue heron eat crayfish. So do other animals, but there are still enough left to lay more eggs to hatch into crayfish to grow up and lay more eggs and so on and on. It's a good thing this happens. It happens to other animals too.

FROGS LAY LOTS OF EGGS

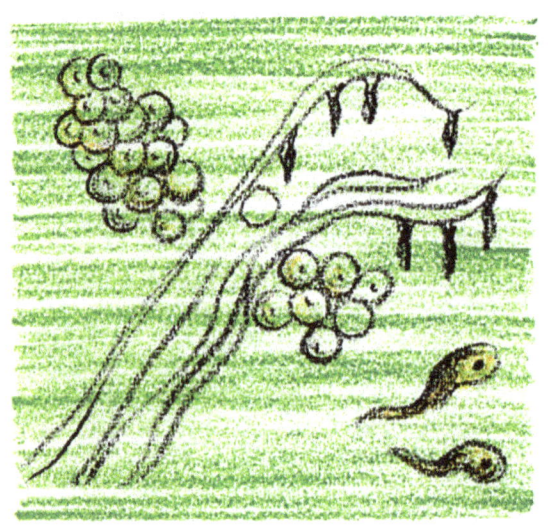

GARTER SNAKES HAVE LOTS OF LITTLE SNAKES

# BUMBLEBEES AND CLOVER AND MICE

Bumblebees by the dozens fly over the red clover that grows in the meadow. You can hear them buzz sometimes before you can see them. The bumblebees and the clover are very important to each other. Now you might not think that bumblebees have anything to do with the mice that live in the meadow. But they do, for if there were no mice in the meadow there probably wouldn't be very many bumblebees, and if there were only a few bumblebees there wouldn't be much clover. Now why do you suppose this can be? Let's see.

Red clover grows from seeds just as many other plants do. The flowers of red clover make the seeds. The dust that is in the red clover flower is called pollen. The pollen must be carried from one flower to another or the flower will not make good seeds. This is where bumblebees come in. They visit the red clover flowers to get this dusty pollen and a sweet juice called nectar. They use the pollen and nectar for food.

Other insects don't visit red clover very much because they are not built to get the nectar. Their tongues are too short. But bumblebees have longer tongues than the other insects and they can reach down, down into the red clover blossoms and sip the nectar. While they are sipping nectar they also get the dusty pollen. If you watch you will see them going from one red clover blossom to another. When they do this they carry the pollen from one flower to another flower and then the flower can make good

seeds. So it's a good thing the bumblebee is built with such a long tongue. If it didn't have this tongue the bumblebee couldn't get the nectar, and it needs nectar and pollen for food. And it's a good thing for the red clover blossom that the bees visit it. If they didn't, there wouldn't be enough seed to make more clover.

But what has this to do with the mice that live in the meadow? Mice live in tunnels in the ground. Here and there, if you go exploring, you will see the holes in the ground where the tunnels are. They live in these tunnels for a while, and then they go somewhere else and make new ones. Bumblebees find these old holes and tunnels, and they are just right for bumblebees to use as homes. So when the mice move out, the bumblebees move in. There are many bumblebee homes in the meadow. If the mice didn't make the holes the bumblebees wouldn't have any places to live because bumblebees are not built for digging holes for themselves.

If there were no bumblebee homes there wouldn't be any bumblebees. If there were no bumblebees, there would be no way for pollen to get from one blossom to another, and if this didn't happen there wouldn't be seeds for next year's clover to grow from.

You are probably surprised at this. Most people are. But when you go exploring in a meadow you are often surprised at the things you discover. Many other animals and plants are partners like this.

# OTHER MEADOWS

Now you see that the animals that live in this meadow are adapted to their environment. If they dig or if they climb or fly or hop they are especially built to do it. If they nibble or if they gnaw or if they chew or sip they are especially built to do it.

The world is full of fine meadows and you know that the best way to explore a meadow is to open the gate and walk in. These are some of the things you might see:

ALONG A WALL YOU MIGHT SEE WOODCHUCKS AND CHIPMUNKS

IN THE GRASS YOU MIGHT SEE GRASSHOPPERS AND CRICKETS

A GREEN SNAKE

IN OR NEAR THE POND YOU MIGHT SEE A RED-WINGED BLACKBIRD IN THE CATTAILS

A WATER STRIDER

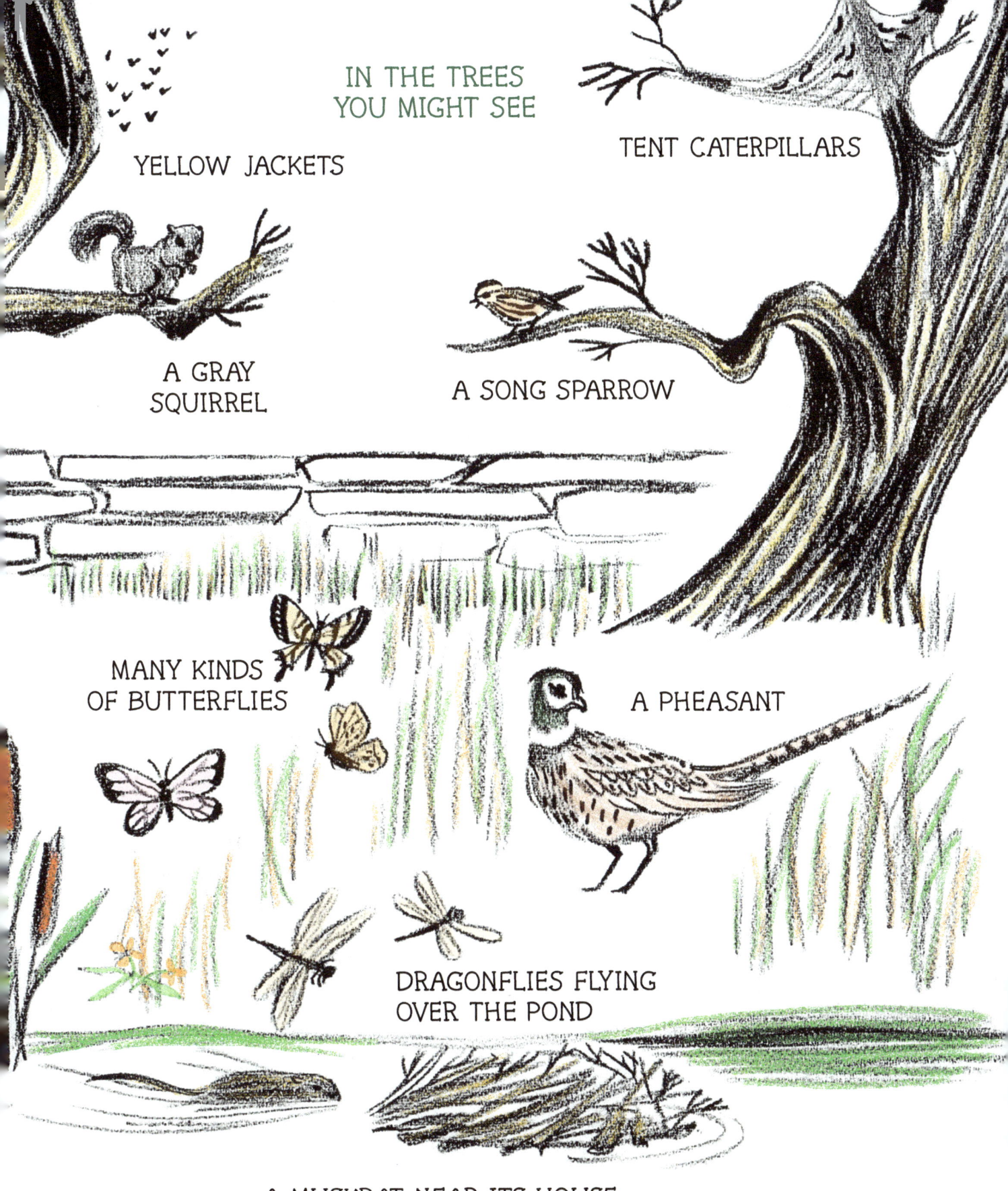

Remember to listen for sounds. Look into the water. Watch the birds and other animals and you will see that they are all adapted to their environment. And while you are walking along you may scare up a rabbit. Who knows? You'll be surprised if you do. So will the rabbit. And maybe you will see bumblebees and red clover and mice. And if you do, maybe you will tell somebody a surprising thing about them.

The *Purple House Press* Nature Study Library is growing, with books being added monthly from authors you'll enjoy. In addition to Glenn Blough and Jeanne Bendick, look for Alice Goudey, Robert McClung, Herbert Zim and more! Check purplehousepress.com for the latest news.

www.ingramcontent.com/pod-product-compliance
Lightning Source LLC
Chambersburg PA
CBHW051355110526
44592CB00024B/2987